MESSAGES from
THE SOUL

MESSAGES from
THE SOUL

*From the thoughts and motives
of the depth of our being*

Vinoa Ebron Wilson

XULON PRESS

Xulon Press
2301 Lucien Way #415
Maitland, FL 32751
407.339.4217
www.xulonpress.com

© 2021 by Vinoa Ebron Wilson

All rights reserved solely by the author. The author guarantees all contents are original and do not infringe upon the legal rights of any other person or work. No part of this book may be reproduced in any form without the permission of the author.

Due to the changing nature of the Internet, if there are any web addresses, links, or URLs included in this manuscript, these may have been altered and may no longer be accessible. The views and opinions shared in this book belong solely to the author and do not necessarily reflect those of the publisher. The publisher therefore disclaims responsibility for the views or opinions expressed within the work.

Unless otherwise indicated, Scripture quotations taken from the King James Version (KJV) – *public domain*.

Paperback ISBN-13: 978-1-6628-1417-4

Ebook ISBN-13: 978-1-6628-1418-1

Dedication

Dedicated with grateful appreciation to my Mom, Dora Ebron-Keyes, for her unwavering love and nurturing spirit.

Mom, you modeled God's Love, had the patience of Job, the compassion of Jeremiah and enough gentle fortitude to raise 14 children in the fear of the Lord.

Thank you, Mom. Your life, for me, is and will always be a living epistle.

Pops, I thank God that you are in Heaven. Our prayers for you never stopped, so when the Lord called you home, we knew you were ready to go. I dedicate this book to you as well. Without you, many things in this book could not have been written. Love you dad!

In remembrance to my dear friend, and daughter in the Lord, Valerie Jenkins, for her constant reminder that God gave me a gift that should be shared with others.

This book is written in memory of your faithful friendship and your walk with Christ to the very end. You will always be remembered.

Lord I said, "I'll go"; now here I stand.
Help me send this blessed book all over the land;
To help some wandering soul find their way to Christ;
Another soul will be set free and gain eternal life.

-written by Vinoa Ebron Wilson

Table of Contents

Thanks xi
Introduction xiii

Messages From The Soul

Don't Blame Jesus 1
Strange Invader 3
My Decision 4
What Are We Here For? 6
Achievement Through Teamwork 9
Do You Know Him? 12
A Soul That Longs For Christ 13
What Then? 15
Live A Life For Him 16
What's The Use? 17
What Did Jesus Do? 18
A God-Fearing Dedicated Man 20
Point Of Contact 21
The Answer To A Burdened Soul 22
Somewhere, Somebody Cares 24
The Believer's Call 25
I Began To Care 26

The Christmas Story

The Christmas Story 29
Will You Be Ready When Jesus Comes Again? 33

Mother's Day

Welcome Address for Mothers 39
Church Mothers 40
A Mother's Day Honor 41

YOU ARE WELCOME

Welcome Address Union 45
Missionary Day Welcome 46

EULOGY CONDOLENCES

Eulogy Consolation 49
There Are Others Who Must Follow 50
Joy Is Coming In The Morning 52
Though Death Comes, Life Must Continue 53
Life's Lessons 55
Are You Ready? 56
Good-Bye World 57
Falling Tears Of The Rain 58
Our Lives Are In His Hands 59
Built to Last 60

MATTERS OF THE HEART

What Is The Gift Of Love? 65
You're The One 66
One Moment 67
I Wish 68
In Need Of A Friend 70
The Friend Who Just Stands By 72

Thanks

Special thanks to my mom, Dora Ebron-Keyes, for saving all my poems throughout the years. Without you, Mom, there would have been no evidence of my writings.

Thank you, Kimberly (Perkins) Russell. Your surprise gift of the compilation of my poetry provided the ultimate inspiration. Kim, I could not have done this without your insight of what my poems would look like in a book format.

To my family, (sisters and brothers), Robert (aka. Bobby), Ronald, Solomon, Melford, Charas, Sgt. Lynwood (aka. Little boy), Glenwood (aka. Big boy/Slim), William, Leroy, Merian, Grace, Delores and Deborah... it was from our lives and our experiences that the Lord inspired me to write these poems. I pray they will be encouragement to all of you.

Last, but not least, to my beloved husband, W. Frank (aka. Chili), and my children, Ivana Monique (aka. Vee, Fire) and Benjamin Preston (aka. BJ, Choze, Ice) ... thank you for always being there for me. I pray these poems will continue to inspire you to keep the faith and never give up on your dreams. Continue to use your gifts for the Lord. I know your writings, too, will touch many lives as you continue to walk in your calling. Remember, we can do all things in Christ who strengthens us.

This is a special thank you to three persistent ladies; my sister, Deborah Ann (Ebron) McDowell, my daughter, Ivana Monique and my daughter-in-love, Mirriam Knight-Wilson, who continued to encourage me to finish this book so others could share in my love of poetry and concern for the souls of men.

Introduction

At age 12, I was traumatized when a gun, fired by a family member, missed my head by a few inches. That incident left me with a severe speech dysfluency. My dysfluency caused me to be shy and nervous about communicating verbally. Since I was unable to verbalize what I wanted to say, I began to do it in writing. I recall one of my English teachers telling me that I should consider being a writer since I was able to express myself so well on paper.

One night, while lying in bed, crying and frightened, I saw a strange figure of a man walk into my room. I thought it was my dad, but there was a bright light shining all around this person. I felt a calmness about him, and my fear turned to excitement. I immediately jumped out of bed and begin writing my first poem, 'Strange Invader.' This poem flowed almost effortlessly from my mind to the paper. From that point on, I carried a pen and paper everywhere I went because I never knew when I would be inspired to write again. When you read the poem entitled 'Strange Invader', my hope is that you will gain some insight into what I experienced that night.

So much of my writing took place while I rode on the subways of New York City, and as I walked the streets of Brownsville, New York. My heart would break as I saw the chaos, trouble, drugs, prostitution, hunger, killing and more, happening on the streets where I had to travel.

I have included poems in this book written by my mom, Dora Keyes-Ebron and my daughter, Ivana Monique. I left the dates on them because of the significance of the moments they were written. Dora's poem, "Will You Be Ready When Jesus Comes?" was dedicated to the Keyes family, as well as her

children. The underlying tone of this poem comes from her burden for their souls.

Ivana Monique's poem, "Built to Last" was written and read on August, 1, 2007 at the Homegoing of her grandmother, Gussie Mae Wilson. There are several poems in my book written by her that I hope will inspire you.

In addition to poetry, I was also given the gift of writing plays. My first Christmas skit, "The Christmas Story", was written November, 6, 1972. I chose to leave the dates on these three writings because they represent milestones in the lives of each writer.

I pray that these messages from my soul will be a blessing to renew your heart, and encourage you on this journey called life.

Messages From The Soul

Don't Blame Jesus

Listen, my friend, I have something to say,
It may help you see the light or may drive your soul away.
But the truth is always right, so please listen to me tell,
How the Lord can help your soul escape the deep, dark pit of hell.

You have gambled, you have cheated, you have lived a life of sin,
You are heading down the path, where, Satan's wrath is at the end.
He has entered in your heart, and he's trying for your soul,
You had better stop right here and let the Lord take control.

What? You say that time is yours for you heard the Lord was dead,
Then who woke you up this morning, helped you rise up from the bed?
And who gave you legs to walk, set your feet upon the ground?
And who gave you food to eat, that in the Frigidaire was found?

No, my friend, don't say you did, for the power is in His hands,
He can breathe the breath of life or death moves at His command.
He can lift you to the highest or can bring your swiftly down,
If it were not for the Lord, you'd be buried in the ground.

But my Lord has the patience, and He's waiting for the day
You realize your heart and soul, from His hands have gone astray.
For He died to save the sinner, and He rose up once again,
He is pleading for the soul that is lost and deep in sin.

Ah! You say it is no use, for you've gone too far to reach;
That is why my Blessed Savior put disciples here to teach.
For through them He brings the words of eternal life to you,
And although you're at the brink, He can help your
soul renew.

But you know the right from wrong, and which way you
want to go,
If you chose the path of sin, then, there's something you
should know.
It was not my Savior's fault that you fell into the pit,
For He made a way for you, and the path was always lit.

If you open up the Bible, and you read John 3:16,
You will sense the Savior's love, and will know just
what I mean.
All you have to do is pray, and be sorry for your sin,
For my Lord is always waiting, pleading you to let Him in.

Even left His words of wisdom, which to heaven is the key;
How to walk, and how to talk, how to live victoriously.
For God sent His only Son, through His death and blood
He frees us;
So, the choice is up to you, but please remember, Don't
Blame Jesus.

Strange Invader

A Stranger just stepped through my door,
His form, majestic, from head to floor.
His hair, like lambs' wool, His face, like the sun;
I must have been dreaming or have just begun.

His feet, shining brass, His eyes, burning fire,
His heart, overflowing, with loving desire.
His arms, are extended, like He's bidding me to come;
His presence, flow of joy and peace, I'm eager to have some.

So, I listened very closely, and I hear this Stranger say:
"My child, you look so weary, so come home, come home today."
"Yes", I said, "I know I'm weary, for at times my strength is gone;
But dear Stranger, guide my journey, pick me up and make me strong.

For You called me to this work, that can only be done through Thee,
So please help me save a soul, that's lost in sin, as was me."
So, this Stranger smiled and said: "journey on, My Words please share.
Spread your love, your joy, compassion, show the world how much I care."

So, I traveled on through life, winning souls as Christ's Crusader,
And most of all, I'm proud to say, that I know this Strange Invader.

My Decision

While wandering through this world, unconcerned and carefree;
These thoughts came to my mind: "what will I really be?
What will I really do, when troubles really press?
What will surely happen, when I the Lord would test?"

Frightened and confused, hurt and in despair,
I ran to Christ my Savior, and uttered a fervent prayer.
He heard my supplication, with a tender voice He said,
"Fear not my dear_____[1] for there's nothing you should dread".

"I have you in My service; I have you in My care;
If you ever have a problem, you know I will be there."
It was then I made a decision, to Christ I will belong,
Through faith, hope and trust, His Will, will make me strong.

My life was then in Him, and He belonged to me;
But burdens began to press, as heavy as can be.
It was then I thought again, "Whom am I to please?
The world with all its sorrows, or my Lord down on my knees?"

But then I heard a voice say, "I alone can save.
The world can offer nothing; I have victory from the grave."
So once again I gave my life, in Him to be complete.
I read my Word, I prayed a prayer and sat at my Savior's feet.

So, when you have a problem, and nowhere else to turn,
There is a blessed Savior, who is dear and quite concerned.
If you want someone to love you, when things are going wrong,

---

[1] Insert Name Here

Remember my decision; choose Christ, He'll make you strong.

What Are We Here For?

As I walk along the streets, as I ride upon the trains,
I can see a sorrow view, of the world that still remains.
As the troubles grow and grow, while the world is
standing still;
Some poor soul is wandering, someone's child is very ill.

As I gather with the crowds, as I listen to them talk;
I can see that many speak, but of the Way, they do not walk.
Souls are searching, looking, seeking for the peace they'll
never find,
'Til they meet the blessed Savior, One who gives them
peace of mind.

Yet I ask you, what is life that we should honor it so dear?
Does it matter if I'm smiling, or my eyes should shed a tear?
Does it matter if I die, and never leave a speck or trace,
Of the person lost in sin, with no mind for saving grace?

Does it matter if I'm naked, have nowhere to lay my head?
Does it matter if I'm hungry, and my children can't be fed?
Yes, you say you are concerned, about the ones who are
lost in sin,
But you do not lift a finger, to let them know they
have a friend.

Why, my friend, must we tarry, when there's so much
work to do?
Are you waiting for the Savior to present some
THING to you?
Makes no sense to sit and wonder, if He'll call you
now, or then.
If you know the blessed Savior, you can see those lost in sin.

For you see, there is a Savior, one who blesses rich and poor.

All we need is ask forgiveness, seek His face, open the door.
He will save you, guide you, keep you, from all hurt, harm or danger.
He's a friend to the friendless, to Him alone, there is no stranger.

He was willing to bear our sorrow, food and shelter He gave to all.
When our burdens press so heavy, He hears our prayers, answers our call.
On this earth He healed the sick, helped the blind and fed the poor.
When His strength began to fail, He prayed a prayer and helped some more.

He's the One that we should follow, one who saves us by His grace;
Had no eyes for white or colored, all to Him was one big race.
But we are proud, too high to follow in such a humble, lowly way.
We find no time to help the sinner, or the time for God today.

We say our lives are in our hands, to rise and shine and have our being,
But my friend, when life is over, we'll find our words didn't mean a thing.
But Christ was born to save the sinner, He never lied, nor did He cheat.
He gave His life upon the cross, they nailed His hands, His precious feet.

He taught us how to say a prayer, when trials seemed to press us down.
He said, we'll see His kingdom come, He said that we would wear a crown.
So, I wonder how can we, whom God has helped from day to day,

Go about our daily tasks and watch our children go astray?

We had our fun and they must too; we say that life will not endure.
If helping others is not our call, then tell me, What Are We Here For?

Achievement Through Teamwork

(Old Song)

This is MY song; this is MY prayer.
This is MY joy; I will NOT share.
This is MY church, MY pastor too.
They belong to ME, and NOT to you.

(New Song)

YOU worked in YOUR church; YOU sang with YOUR choirs;
YOU had all YOUR friends, and all YOUR stand-byers.
The things that YOU did were praise for YOURself,
But it is now time to get off of YOUR shelf.

We have been divided a little too long;
It's now time for us to sing a brand-new song.
Let us work together to achieve the best;
To help OUR community find peace and rest.

For many are watching those living in Christ;
Not only what WE say, but also OUR life.
WE have a goal, let's be on OUR way,
Though trials may come, OUR faith will not stray.

For it is OUR joy, and it is OUR hope,
To please OUR Savior, to widen the scope.
Of life that's eternal and can only be,
Given from the Father for ALL to see.

For in OUR Savior, there's love and there's trust;
To do HIS work, HE uses US.
OUR hands, are HIS Hands, to do HIS will;
OUR feet, are HIS feet, to climb the rugged hill.

OUR tongues, is HIS tongue, to speak HIS Holy Word;
So many can hear, what They have never heard,
Of how OUR Savior, so humble and low,
Died to save US, HIS love He did show.

HE worked as a team and WE must work too;
To help accomplish what HE wants US to do.
Achievement thru teamwork is OUR motto this year;
So, let's work, let's pray, let's love and let's share.

For this is OUR future, and it is OUR goal,
To help OUR community, the Gospel unfold.
And only together can this come about,
With no one to stop US and no one to doubt.

So, if YOU'RE not with US, or YOU really don't care,
Because of YOUR doubt or because of YOUR fear;
Because YOU are selfish, because YOU'RE too proud,
Step out of the boat, but please don't be loud.

For many are searching for truth and for peace;
So, if YOU'RE not with US, YOUR mouth should then cease.
For WE are determined, OUR work to achieve,
And only thru teamwork, WE do believe;

To get what WE want, takes fasting and prayer,
Money and love, plus sorrow and care.
Yet working together, and not all alone,
Will save US some hair and some skin on OUR bone.

So, open YOUR hearts, and help US to gain,
The community that all of US wish to obtain.
Still, many will fight US until they all see,
The love, joy and peace in OUR community.

Built by Disciples, the followers of Christ,
Working together and living the life;

Helping the poor to get what THEY need,
Through teamwork and faith, WE WILL SUCCEED.

Do You Know Him?

Have you heard of the way Jesus made the blind to see?
How He left His home in glory, bled and died on Calvary?
How He arose from the dead, with all power in His hand;
Sitting on the throne, angels moved at His command?

Have you heard of the way; He makes all burdens seem to roll?
How He opens up shut doors, like they were a paper scroll?
Yes, He is the One to serve; He's the answer to our prayer.
When it seems that you're alone, He's the One who is always there.

Have you heard of the Savior, who cleanses us from sin?
Extending out His arms, pleading us to enter in.
Assuring all who will, you'll find happiness and peace,
In the fold of the Lord, our joy will never cease.

But to have this joy and peace, we must all be pure and clean,
Not a spot, or a blemish on our soul must be seen.
For it's easy for a camel through a needle's eye to go,
Then for any sinful soul to enter heaven's gates, you know.

So, my children, let us travel, and let's see what we can do,
To help some wayward sinner find this life eternal too.
For we all will share the joys, and our sorrows soon will dim,
With our life in Christ our Savior, I ask you now, "Do You Know Him?"

A Soul That Longs For Christ

I'm a joker, in a gang, happy and carefree,
But deep down in my heart, I am sad as I can be.
I drink to keep from crying, I smoke to look quite big;
The dope I take, the dance I do, all make me hip, you dig!

My friends, they stick beside me, when my pockets are filled with dough;
But when my pockets are empty, I have nowhere to go.
I've robbed, I've cheated, I've lied, was shot and left to die;
I'm scared, I'm empty, tormented, I've done more than meets the eye.

Walked in the rain to hide my tears from heartbreak of some sort;
My life was based on false pretense, I had no real support.
I've done quite a lot in my lifetime, experienced no joy at all;
Instead of feeling big and strong, it made me feel quite small.

I may appear quite happy too; my heart may seem content,
But deep within there is no joy, my life and soul lament.
I'm tired now, I need some peace, I've had my life long fun;
I'm worried now about myself, and the things that I have done.

A friend of mine, stopped by my house, to pray with me today;
She told me of a Savior, Who, could take my burdens away.
But, I'm afraid to approach the One, with such power in His hands;
For if I slip just one more time, my soul He may demand.

I want to really follow Him, how bad I long to know;
Of how He fills your heart with joy, when sorrows start to grow.

But how do I, a sinner, in this world find an escape;
Into the hands of Christ the Savior, a new life to re-shape?

I realize I must find the way to Christ the royal King;
I do not want to die in sin, for death will then me sting.
Please, help me find this narrow way, the way that
leads to life;
I'm lost, I'm sad, I'm weary, I'm a soul that longs for Christ.

What Then?

Now and then you'll find a traveler,
Now and then you'll find a friend;
On this pathway to Damascus,
Only few will enter in.

Remember how the Bible said:
"The destruction road is very wide?
Many souls have entered it,
Many souls will also die.

But the narrow road to heaven,
Is a rugged road, you see?
And the few that find the Son light,
Forever live eternally."

So, dear soul, do not tarry;
Hasten now before the end.
When my Lord speaks words of sorrow:
"Depart from Me", dear soul, WHAT THEN?

Live A Life For Him

If you're lonely, write a poem.
If you're happy, sing a song.
But no matter how you feel,
All your soul to Him must yield.

If you're lost, nowhere to go,
There is one who loves us so.
He's forever lurking near;
He always sees so do not fear.

The aches and pains that we may feel;
My God is able to help us heal.
He will help us bear our load,
Down this steep and rugged road.

Life in Him will be complete;
If we will kneel down at His feet.
He's the one we need the most;
Father, Son, and Holy Ghost.

Are you surprised there is a One?
Brighter than the morning sun?
Never mind when troubles grow;
Lean on Jesus, He'll let you know,

He is three and three in one,
He's the Father and the Son.
Not forgetting the Holy Ghost,
Try your best to please Them most.

What's The Use?

When burdens press you very low,
And never seem to let you go;
You start to think, deep down within:
"What's my reward in the end?"

Father against you, mother is too;
Some in the church are even untrue.
Stones in your way, wherever you turn;
Why are you suffering, what will you earn?

Then it happens, those times of abuse,
And you wonder within: "what's the use?"
"What's the use of suffering, for a God unseen?"
A God someone felt, a soul He redeemed."

"What's the use of caring, when others don't care?"
"What's the use of sharing, when others don't share?"
"Why should you witness to those lost in sin?"
"Why should you worry whether they make it in?"

Yet "faith is the substance of things hoped for;"
You remember that passage and ask for more, of
Faith, Hope and Love, that's what you need;
To help you follow, as Jesus leads.

You then have a hope that will never fail;
A hope deep within that will always prevail.
You look toward the heavens; for your chains have come loose,
And you're glad you never uttered, "What's the Use?"

What Did Jesus Do?

What did Jesus do, when he was buked and scorned?
What did Jesus do, when they placed a crown of thorns?
Not a groan was uttered, not a tear was shed,
As His pure blood dripped from His aching head.

In His perfect heart was love, He extended it to all,
For He knew there would come a day, when we would
have to call;
Upon His precious name to be delivered from all fear,
Sin, sickness and pain, sorrow and care.

He was led to Calvary, crucified on a hill,
In a tomb they laid his body, rolled a stone and placed a seal.
On the third Sunday He rose, with all power in His hand,
Conquered death, and gave us life, angels moved at
His command.

All who wish to follow Him, in their hearts must always be,
Completely His, just surrender all, in order to be free.
Not, soul to Satan and mouth to Christ, for that is
not the way;
To enter into Heaven, you must yield your soul today.

For those who say: "I belong to Him," and lie and steal
and cheat;
Eternal life is not their home, they live life in defeat.
For on this journey, there's just one way, for us to
find our home;
The path of righteousness and peace, the way that Christ
has shown.

For I, myself, did seek the Way, the Truth, the Life, the Cross;
Where Jesus died to save my soul from sin and eternal loss.

So, when I'm tossed, buked and scorned, and deeply burdened too,
Then I can answer the question with confidence – WHAT DID JESUS DO?

A God-Fearing Dedicated Man

There once was a man so frail and so meek;
He was anointed by God, but his voice was still weak.
Then one day the Gospel was brought to his ears;
He fell on his knees and to God cried in tears.

"My Father forgive me, and cleanse me from sin."
Christ anointed his tongue, healed his body from within.
So now this old creature whose life became new;
Was determined and dedicated, faithful and true.

When called by the Lord, he answered: "I'll go!"
"I'll preach Your Gospel and let the world know;
That You died to save us, and You rose once again;
Extending Your arms, pleading all to come in."

So, this dedicated man, so thin yet so strong;
Step out of the world, to Christ he belonged.
Though trials and troubles pressed hard every day;
This dedicated man continued to pray.

He was given a flock to lead and to teach;
Each Monday through Friday, and Sunday he preached.
This dedicated man, so determined, and true;
Vowed to the Lord, His will he would do.

Whenever the flock had burdens to bear,
This dedicated man was so willing to share.
He was one of God's best, as he stood before all;
Believing that God would hear when he called.

So, whenever you look for a man that is true,
A man that will preach the real gospel to you;
One that is faithful, and does all he can;
Think of the God-fearing, Dedicated Man.

Point Of Contact

I longed to do a service, a service I longed to do;
To please my blessed Savior, my Savior kind and true.
I longed to help some sinner, a sinner I longed to show;
The pathway to salvation, the Christ who loves him so.

Yet how could I who stuttered, on every word I said;
Teach someone, some sinner, the Way that Christ has led.
They will not listen to me; for I'm hard to understand;
So, Savior, help me speak and explain Your perfect plan.

Prayer, is the answer, it is the key to my every need.
When I pray to Christ, my Savior, His Spirit will intercede.
If it seems He does not answer, as I pray both day and night;
I know that He is with me and I won't give up the fight?

In my heart, I know He's near me, and He hears me
when I pray;
Even when the stuttered words seemed to worsen every day.
But then I heard a whisper: "My child, your faith does lack."
"Just trust in me and lean on me; as your only point
of contact."

So, since I had the answer, my faith I did release;
To Jesus, my blessed Redeemer, my faith He did increase.
And when I speak of His promise, for others to receive;
I know that my personal witness, will help them to believe;

The message of God's love, His care, concern, in fact;
The witness of my faith in Him, Christ Jesus, My Point
of Contact.

The Answer To A Burdened Soul

Lord, I said I'll go, but I'm still standing here.
Deep inside I feel like crying, but I cannot shed a tear.
My heart, it is so heavy, for Your will I have not done;
The battle is still raging, and my soul is on the run.

It's because I feel so weak, and my soul is in despair.
I've allowed the circumstances, in my life to turn to fear.
When I say, I have no time, I realize that's no excuse;
For it only takes a second, just to put my faith to use.

"Well, my child, you said you'll go, and to Me, you surrendered all.
Don't you know I'm always here and I'll hear you when you call?
Many souls are lost in sin and they are dying every day;
There is really no time to tarry, I will hear you when you pray."

"So, fear not, for I am with you and no harm will come your way.
For I, your blessed Savior will guide you now and every day.
So, continue, please don't worry; this is not the time to quit.
Rise and be upon your journey, this is not the time to sit."

"You cannot experience joy when you know your work's undone.
When you answered: 'Lord I'll go', then your battle had just begun.
Do not lack at any point, for tomorrow's not the key.
I am knocking at the door to give life eternally."

"But, if you decide to linger, while the souls around you stand;
I have another servant, who will move at My command.

But it's you that I have called, and it's you I want to use,
For you're young and at the point where my flock will
not refuse;"

"To obey a faithful servant, whom I know has tried their best;
Off and on there will be trials; off and on you'll pass the test.
But dear soul, you must continue, for your journey
will not end;
Until all my wandering children, at the gate have entered in."

Somewhere, Somebody Cares

As I was riding on the train,
I took a stroll down memory lane.
The consciousness of a lonely heart;
That dares itself from this world depart.

What manner of thought can this possibly be?
In the mind of one so loving and free?
In giving all the help, you can,
To every woman, girl, boy and man.

It's not from God, and that's for sure;
For God will help you to endure.
He's the giver of life's greatest treasures;
And every ounce of love, He measures.

So, dispel the thought of the lonely snares;
For on this earth, somewhere, somebody cares.

The Believer's Call

God called him on a cool noonday. "Come preach for me,"
he heard Him say.
"Some soul is drifting off in sin; go tell them I will be
their friend."

And so he answered to the call of that great wondrous voice.
So every creature great and small, could love, live
and rejoice.

He labored night, he labored day, sometimes both tossed
and driven;
Yet in his heart, in every way, God's Word he had been given.

For many souls were bound in sin, and only God could loose;
The hurt, the pain within their hearts, the nights filled
with abuse.

And so, he traveled on and on, no matter what the weather;
And in his heart, he kept a song, 'these lives would
live forever'.

So, let's rejoice for the Son of Man, one night in a
stable small;
Was born to die in a foreign land, to send out a believer's call.

I Began To Care

I watched the trains go rushing by,
And planes take off into the sky.
The buses rolled down lonely streets,
And taxis stopped for tired feet.

I saw a child with smiles of glee;
Someone's 'hello' was said to me.
Yet as I turned the corner near;
T'was then my heart began to care.

I saw a child, cold, wet from rain.
Her hair just hung like a horse's mane.
I quickly took her in my arms;
To shield her from this world of harm.

She looked at me with tender eyes;
I felt her fear, I heard her cries.
I gave her all the love I could;
The love, I felt a mother would.

And just within that little time;
All MY cares were left behind.
For this world would never see;
The smile she gave to comfort me.

And I shall never forget that day;
Walking, wondering what to say,
To a child so filled with fear;
I just thank God I began to care.

The Christmas Story

The Christmas Story

Narrator: Sing we now of Christmas, sing we here Noel;
T'is the Christmas story, I'm about to tell.
T'was an angel sent, down from Heaven above,
To tell the blessed Mary, a child she would bear with love.

Mary: Oh, what radiant beauty, stands before me bright?
Who is this, prey tell me, in such wondrous white?

Angel: Fear not, my dear Mary, in God's sight art thou;
Found with love and mercy, humbly as you bow.
In thy womb conceived, the Christ child has been placed.
All the world will bless thee, through His saving grace.

Mary: How can I conceive, one who knows no man?

Angel: Only through The Spirit, will you fill this great command.

Mary: Be it so, dear angel. His servant I shall be.
Tis a blessed privilege to bear such one as He.

Narrator: And so, the seed was planted, into the virgin fair;
And God dispatched an angel, now a man he must prepare.
For Mary was a virgin, and God, He knew too well;

That people's talk, can prove so wrong, when understanding fails.
And so, the angel journeyed, to Joseph's house he flew.
For God had chosen Joseph, to be the husband new.

Angel: Arise, dear humble servant, for God has seen in thee;
An understanding heart, that no one else could see.
With child, there lives a virgin, whom God has looked upon;
To bear the blessed Savior, in a world lost and undone.
She is the virgin, Mary, and yet no man has she;
And so, with God's great blessings, you will her husband be.

Joseph: To God, be the glory, to have His work fulfilled;
Through one that's so unworthy, yet in His sight I kneel.
I'll render Him my service, to wed the virgin fair;
And ease the talking burdens, as she, with child shall bear.

Narrator: And so, the humble servant, arose quite instantly;
To fill his call of duty, the angel said to be.
And when the call for taxes was placed on every head,
A journey for the Blessed child, with mother, now was led.
With Joseph by her side and Jesus in her womb;

They traveled long, they traveled hard, yet could not find a room;
To bear the heavy burden, that now, within Mary pressed;
A stable was the only place to give her body rest.
Then through the air, a song went out, as shepherds watched by night; The voice of angels singing sweet, a star that shone so bright.

Shepherds: "What can this mean?"

Narrator: The shepherds said as they fell to the ground.

Angel: "Be not afraid, a child is born, in Bethlehem 'tis found.
He'll save His people from their sins, He'll draw all men He said,
If they will only lift Him up, go seek the Savior's bed."

Narrator: And so, the shepherds journeyed on, the star did lead the way;
And took its anchor in the sky, O'er Bethlehem did stay.
And still the star was seen afar, by Wise Men in the East;
And they, too, journeyed on to see just what this star released.
And when for them, the star did stand above the stable roof;
They journeyed on and entered in and there they found the proof.
For in a manger, laid a babe, just wrapped in swaddling clothes;

A light that shone about His head and all around Him glowed.
They gave Him gold, myrrh, frankincense, and all that you could see;
Yet no one knew the truth behind this Blessed child to be.
But we, today, can understand just why this child was born;
On that bright blessed Christmas day, in Bethlehem that morn.
He came to save this sinful world, was born for you and me;
And through His death, He bore our sins way back on Calvary.
And so, today, we give our thanks, in honor we do sing;
All glory to the Blessed child and praise be to our King.

Written by Vinoa Ebron Wilson
(November 6, 1972)

Will You Be Ready When Jesus Comes Again?

(Dedicated to the Keyes Family and Friends)

In that great triumphant morning, when the trump of God shall sound;
T'will be the climax of salvation; Christ, our King, will soon be crowned.
No man knows the day or hour, nor the angels up in heaven;
God the Father has set the time, don't try to guess one through eleven.

Christ may come at any time, the archangels herald back;
"You will never make it in, if in your heart HIS SON you lack.
You must open up your heart, let the loving Savior in.
Believe, confess and then repent, humbly bow and come to Him."

Our God's love is a perfect love, He gave His Son to set us free;
Resurrected, conquered every foe, went to prepare a place for you and me.
Jesus promised to come back, for His bride so bright and fair;
To inhabit the blessed land, He prepared for us up there.

A land so pure all paved with gold, and gates so pearly white;
His Church to live, this is our goal, to rest in His delight.
Jesus' promises are true, and on His Word, you can rely;
Read your Bible every day, His Words of truth you can't deny.

Jesus' final counsel to His disciples, "Go ye" with power to preach;

Into all the nations round the world, my people, every-
where to reach.
Baptizing them who will believe, in the blessed Trinity;
I came that they might have new life. I came to set the
captive free.

Behold, He was taken up to heaven, while His disciples
gazed in awe;
Out of their sight, the clouds received Him, as He vanished,
they all saw.
"Why stand ye gazing up in heaven?", two men clothed in
white, did say;
"This same Jesus taken up from you, in like manner, will
return one day.

"Unexpected He will come, T'is doom to the careless and
unconcern;
But the faithful are prayerfully looking and awaiting the
Lord's return.
In the glory of His Father, on the clouds, Jesus will come;
With ten thousand of His saints, to judge the deeds that we
have done."

Lo, the sky will be a blazed, with shining angels, glory be;
The awesome splendor of Jesus, visible, will dazzle eyes for
all to see.
In the air, caught up to meet Him, all the people
that are free;
From mortal to immortal change, to the City of God we
will flee.

No more sickness, pain, or death; No more crying for
us up there;
For in the likeness of King Jesus, in His countenance we
will share.
There, we will reign as Kings and Priests, with a crown of
righteousness;

There to live with Him forever, there to be forever blessed.

So, my family and my friends, let us run this race to win;
Be not terrified by His coming, flee His wrath, and turn from sin.
Running to the rocks and mountains, crying in fright to fall on me;
Hide me from the wrath of God, for His face I cannot see.

So, let's be real, not professing Christians, living only in godly frame;
In desperation before God pleading, 'Lord didn't I prophesy in Thy name?'
"Depart from me, I never knew you," the Judge's reply will be so firm;
"In the lake of fire and brimstone, GO, with Satan and his angels BURN!"

"Well done thy good and faithful servant", to the faithful He shall say;
The battle's won, our hope of glory, a song of victory shall be sung that day.
In my conclusion, my friends and family, whosoever will, let him come;
Drink of the water of life freely; enter into your joyful home.

The night is far spent, the day is at hand...
WILL YOU BE READY WHEN JESUS COMES AGAIN?

Written by Dora Ebron-Keyes
(Mom) (July 2002)

Mother's Day

Welcome Address for Mothers

To all of the mothers who are gathered here,
We extend our love and bring you cheer.
In the welcome today, we want you to know,
Our love for you all will continue to grow.

Through laughter, through tears, through sorrow and all,
The things we experienced in Spring and in Fall.
You cooked and you cleaned, you caused us to see,
What a life within Christ could turn out to be.

With all of life's changes, you stayed close and dear,
And taught us to worship, to love and to share.
What more could we say to make your hearts glow?
Well, mothers, today we are all here to show...

How much you are welcomed, how much you are loved,
And shower you with blessings God sends from above.
May God ever bless you and cause you to be,
Forever remembered, throughout eternity.

Church Mothers

The mothers of the church, who are they?
They are mothers who labor and mothers who pray.

They are mothers who suffer and in reverse,
They are mothers who bless whom others curse.

They are mothers who lift up souls to God;
They are mothers who spare not the chastening rod.

They are mothers of patience and mothers of love,
Mothers of faith sent down from above.

They are mothers we love and mothers we cherish;
They are mothers who teach us so we will not perish.

These are the mothers whom God will bless,
And crown their efforts with success.

A Mother's Day Honor

We are here to honor mothers, I'm so glad that you
have come;
To join us in this service, where you know you are welcome.
For mothers are responsible for keeping us in line,
A scolding might not do the job; you know what's
next in mind.

A mother in the church, has an important job to do;
For many of the younger girls are looking up to you.
To tell them how to live a life in Christ and in the home,
To teach them how to dress themselves, their hair, to
keep it comb.

A mother must show love and care, when burdens
press her so;
Her feelings may be hurt sometimes, but no one is to know.
For somewhere in your very midst, a child is watching you;
Within her heart she has a thought: "I want to be like
her, too."

So, live a life each day and night, at home and everywhere,
So, children whether great or small, will know that you
are there;
To guide them in the way that's right, when they are in
the wrong,
Your life alone can help them sing a new and heavenly song.

Now dear mothers, I must close, but you truly all look sweet,
And since this is your special day, let's stand upon our feet;
And thank God for this special time which was set
aside to show,
That mothers are the sweetest beings in Christ to
come to know.

You Are Welcome

Welcome Address Union

We thank the Lord for another year,
We are able to gather here to share;
The joys of a Union, its sorrows, and love,
Expecting a blessing from above.

So, I'm here to let you know
You're welcome to help our Union grow.
You're welcome to sing, you're welcome to look,
You're welcome to eat the food we cook.

You're welcome to come and take a peek,
Of the joys we share throughout the week.
You're welcome to share our homes and beds,
And feast on the Word of God that's fed.

But let's not forget the reason why
We're gathered together to continue to tie;
The bonds of love that can ever be
Weaved in this Union for all to see.

Missionary Day Welcome

We have gathered to worship, one and all,
So, please listen to this welcome call.
Our Missionary Day is here at last;
Let us celebrate the work that's passed.

You know you are welcome from far and near,
To make this day the best this year.
You are welcome to stay until the very end;
You are welcome to meet a newfound friend.

You are welcome to praise, our risen King,
With hymns of psalms, Hosannas sing.
You are welcome to thank the ones that's here
For working hard to bring some cheer;

To the sick, the needy, and maybe a friend;
To the hungry, the homeless, those at wits end.
You are welcome to help us feed the poor
And show them the way to an open door.

When you heard the voice of God in your heart
On foreign soil you did your part;
To bring a smile to a long-lost soul
Whom God has saved, and now made whole.

So, let's celebrate on this Missionary Day,
To show our love in some small way.
To the ones we know who've done their best
To make a life content and blessed.

Eulogy Condolences

Eulogy Consolation

"Ashes to ashes, dust to dust", once again we hear them say,
But my Savior, God Almighty, died that we may live today.
For our bodies are His temple, where His Spirit always dwells.
Once the breath of life is taken, let us pray that all is well.

For our Spirit takes a journey, Heaven or Hell is the key.
Will we live forever happy or tormented eternally?
And our family, will they wonder, if we made it in the end...
Did our lives speak of the promise, of our Savior, our Lord, and Friend?

We all know that God is love, and in Him we are complete.
If we live for Christ the Savior, up in Heaven we shall meet.
We will gather around the Throne of our Savior, so bright and fair,
There to dwell with Him forever, no more sorrow, no more care.

So, let us live as God commanded, in the Word of God we stand.
We will all meet up in heaven, there to live in Glory Land.

There Are Others Who Must Follow

Your heart aches within, as you read this solemn poem.
There's sorrow all around and a slow absorbing song.
Then you think of the past, and all the things that you've tried,
To keep your children focused on heaven's gates that open wide.

Yet, you know that some will wander, faraway, for they do feel,
They can conquer all the drinking, all the smoking, and the pill.
So, in sorrow, as you view them, in a coffin cold and dim;
In your heart, you cry out, 'Jesus', if only they had accepted Him.

But the devil stole this soul, took a life just in its' prime;
They were young and out of reach, wrapped in sin and all its crime.
Yet there is no time to cry, weep or mourn, the day is gone;
There are others who must follow down the path before the dawn.

So do not sit alone and gloat about the sorrow deep within,
There are others you must save from the grasps of Satan's sin.
Don't give up, there's work to do and other souls that must be won,
For Christ, our Savior, gave His life when we were lost and undone.

"Look to the hills" the Bible says, the help for us has come at last.

For Christ has conquered o'er the grave, and death for us is in the past.
So, rejoice as others seek to find the path of joy and love,
There are others who WILL follow as you point them to heaven above.

Joy Is Coming In The Morning

My Lord, I am weak, and it seems I cannot stand.
This pencil that I hold seem so heavy in my hand.
The life in my body seems to drain day by day,
But I thank You, Lord, for giving me these words to say.

I am happy for the chance to lift my worship unto Thee,
And to serve a risen Savior who gave His life for one like me.
For my Lord, He was found worthy, to bear that rugged cross;
On the hilltop of Gethsemane, in a world that was so lost.

He healed the dumb, He helped the deaf, gave us all His saving grace.
The blind did see, the lame did walk as they looked upon His face.
He came from heaven to open the way, for whosoever will;
Through truth and life, the price He paid, His purpose to fulfil.

And when our burdens press us, that it seems we cannot stand,
Look to the hills and call His name, He is there to take our hand.
Though trials come, we need not fear for in His Word we do abide;
In strength and power, we conquer all, in His Spirit we confide.

We must remember, full joy will come, when all our work is done.
We will reign with Him in heaven, the battle fought, the victory won.
We will sing and praise our Savior and forever we'll adore,
The life eternal, He has promised, to give to us forever more.

Though Death Comes, Life Must Continue

I've come to the end of the road.
My burdens, my cares, and my load;
Are all taken away from me now.
Praise God, I am heavenly bound.

Yet I wonder as I lie on my back;
Many times, my faith I did lack.
Have I helped some poor soul find the way?
Did I do all my best every day?

Can my sisters and brothers all be,
So proud they had a sister like me?
Can my Pastor, as he speaks before all,
With a smile, say I answered God's call?

Then I wonder about daddy again;
Did he have a chance to get in?
Did he lead the family astray?
Or all turned to God to obey?

Melford, Solomon, Leroy and Grace,
Did they join this heavenly race?
How is Charas, the faithful of all;
Is he still answering God's call?

I am sure that the Lord will provide,
And He knows who will walk by His side.
He will guide you up and down hill,
So, continue to do His sweet will.

And one day, you too will have rest.
You've finished the job, past the test.
For only in Christ can you last,
And only through Christ can you pass.

Life's Lessons

Ashes to ashes, dust to dust, to the ground we must return.
When life's lessons are completed, what exactly did we learn?

That the body was a temple where the Spirit did abide.
Once the breath of life is taken, your Spirit crossed the other side.

Heaven or Hell, only God will know, where the soul will find relief;
Is it burning, forever crying, or resting at the Savior's feet?

The choice is yours, so please beware of what you say and what you do.
You can live a life of sin, or a life in God anew.

Are You Ready?

Sorrows may come, but that soon shall past.
Tears will be shed, but that too won't last.
The pain in your heart seems to pierce very deep,
While you view your dear loved one, fallen asleep.

Weep all we may, there is nothing we can do;
To bring back that loved one who has bid us adieu.
For they suffered on this earth, filled with aches and with pains.
Now their soul is at rest beneath the altar of remains.

Yet their death was just a sign, which we all must stop and see,
For the angel that took them, soon will come for you and me.
So, accept the Lord today and no longer will you roam.
When it comes your time to go, you'll be ready to go home.

Are you ready? Yes, I'm ready, I can shout with jubilee;
With the angels up in glory, bowing down on bended knee.

Good-Bye World

Goodbye world you're not our home, we are just passing through.
That includes mother, father, brother, and sister too.

Though this journey up to heaven is a rugged path to trod,
It is only through a form of death; we'll see the face of God.

So dear loved ones do not weep, for we too will have to pass
From this earth of toil and trouble, to a land of peace at last.

Where our sorrows all will end and with Christ,
we'll gladly be
Swallowed in the arms of love, there to live eternally.

So, remember as you travel down this road to follow Christ,
At the end is joy forever, you will have eternal life.

Falling Tears Of The Rain

Tonight, the tears are falling,
Crying for the life that is lost.
Gently they fall comforting the ground,
And by morning, have turned to frost.

Yet the sadness is not a human feeling,
Only nature can feel the pain.
For tonight those falling tears
Are falling tears of the rain.

The trees are filled with water.
The streets are wet with gloom.
Even while families are sitting at home,
The tears of sadness fill the room.

The feeling of grief that is felt
Can drive any person insane.
For the pain of a loved one's death
Are falling tears of the rain.

Written by Ivana Monique
(daughter)

Our Lives Are In His Hands

The day has gone; a new day is dawning;
Some may open their eyes to a brand-new morning.
Others may sleep, till the trumpet is sound,
Not in their bed, but in the ground.

Yet, if we awake, let's remember to pray,
To thank the Lord for this bright new day.
Our blood running warm, we're able to walk;
Our tongue very loose, we're able to talk.

For many had fallen to sleep last night,
But their family awoke in a terrible fright.
Realizing their daughter, or maybe their son,
Had finished their work, their day is now done.

Yes, mother and father, sister and brother,
We all must remember to love one another.
But don't forget the blessings received,
Being able to rise and do as you please.

But when your time comes, and surely it must,
Let within your heart be pure and be just.
For in heaven, a new home, our souls will then share,
With brothers and sisters, from far and from near.

So, let us remember, that when we arise;
And when we are able to open our eyes,
Our limbs are still limber; our tongue is still free,
Our thanks and our hopes and our lives all should be,

Placed in the hands of the One we hold dear;
The One who is able to remove doubt and fear.
And thank Him each morning, and praise Him each night,
Till Heaven's in view and Hell's out of sight.

Built to Last

Our home was where lasting memories were made;
A place we found comfort in a world full of pain.
Where a strong foundation in Christ was laid,
And weakness was replaced with strength gained.

Our home was full of wisdom and contagious laughter,
As words of edification flowed from her mouth.
The love you received was felt for many days after,
Because the love in our home was impossible to doubt.

Our home could change a heart filled with resentment,
And you would always count on her to be there.
Her words could fill any person with complete contentment,
As she prayed powerful, life-altering prayers.

Our home went after the souls of those who were lost,
And would not allow anyone to perish in sin.
She preached the Word of God to others at all costs,
Walking in her calling as a true fisherman.

Our home had a captivating, contagious spirit
That left a fragrance on all who entered the door.
Sound teaching was given to all with ears to hear it,
Filled with encouragement and support to restore.

Our home weathered many storms over the years,
Countless obstacles and trials were faced.
But the foundation on which our home stood was clear,
Rooted in God and filled with unwavering faith.

Our home was the epitome of a virtuous woman of God,
And her children still arise and call her blessed.
She passed on the torch, so in her path we trod,
Until our time comes for our eternal rest.

Our home now rests peacefully in the arms of Jesus Christ.
And although the time spent with us passed so fast,
The memory of our loving home will continue for life,
Because the legacy of our home was built to last.

Written by Ivana Monique
(August 1, 2007)

Madear...Thank you for your legacy. Thank you for the life you lived, the love you gave, and the house you built. A house of faith on which our family will stand for generations to come. You built your hope on Christ, and because of that, the "House" you built was built to last forever. I love you... See ya later.

"It is like a person building a house who digs deep and lays the foundation on solid rock. When the floodwaters rise and break against that house, it stands firm because it is well built." – LUKE 6:48 (NLT)

Matters of the Heart

What Is The Gift Of Love?

What is love that we should care
How other people treat us here?
Our parents surely must have known,
For in our lives their love was shown.

Love is sharing and giving away
Our heart, ourselves from day to day.
Love is God and God is Love,
He is our example sent from Heaven above.

Love can place you in dangerous spots,
Or Love can help you connect the dots;
To the heart of one who would always care,
And longs to draw you ever near.

Love is a gift that comes from God.
Love lights the path where we've always trod.
Love gives life, young and free,
God will send Love to walk with thee.

So, listen now and learn something new;
Find the right mate, you will never be blue.
Your love will continue for many years,
Through storms and trials, through hurt and tears.

I must end now, but I hope you know;
The longer you wait, the stronger you grow.
If hurt, your heart will never fret,
'Cause you did nothing you would soon regret.

Hold on to Love and you soon will find,
A companion from God who is one of a kind.
Happy forever and forever you'll be,
Glad that you listened to little old me.

You're The One

You're the One I first laid eyes on,
The One who became so very dear.
The One I share my every thought with,
As well as my experiences, dreams and fears.

You're the One who believed in me
Even when I didn't believe in myself.
The One who encouraged my every endeavor
To achieve all happiness and wealth.

You're the One who's proven to be so true;
The only One who stayed right by my side.
For it was you who helped me make it through,
When I thought there was no way I could ever survive.

You're the One I can proudly call my friend,
For you as well have confided in me.
There is just one thing I've failed to share;
There is just one thing you've failed to see.

You're the One who's been the One
And although you never even knew,
You're the One I've always loved,
I only wish I could've been your One, too.

Written by Ivana Monique
(daughter)

One Moment

I look forward to every moment I have to spend with you;
For it's when we're together that my every dream comes true.
From being in your arms, wrapped in the tightest embrace;
To the alluring smile I see when I gaze upon your face.

In that moment, every care disappears from my mind;
As I focus on your every touch, so loving, sensual, and kind;
Every inch of my body tingles when you whisper in my ear,
Giving me a feeling of relief from just knowing you're near.

Every kiss from your lips, leaves me mesmerized;
Deep into your eyes, I am left hypnotized.
Sharing and bonding in ways that I will no other;
Knowing in my heart, I want no other lover.

Hoping you'll see in my eyes what my heart is trying to say.
Searching my thoughts for the right words to make you stay.
For in that moment, I belong to you and you belong to me.
In that moment, things are how I wish they could always be.

Written by Ivana Monique
(daughter)

I Wish

I just got the news that you left today.
How I wish I could've been there to say goodbye.
To embrace you once more before sending you on your way,
To see you smile when you say, "I love you" with that familiar sigh.

I wish I could thank you for the wisdom and knowledge you gave,
For loving me despite knowing all there was to know.
For taking care of me when I thought my world would cave;
For all the times I pulled away, but you never let me go.

I wish I could tell you how happy you made me,
How wonderful I always felt in your presence.
How your contagious laughter filled everyone with glee,
How I enjoyed sitting for hours with you just to reminisce.

I wish I could still run to you when my heart is broken,
And feel you wipe the flowing tears from my cheek.
I wish I could feel comfort from each word spoken,
In the way that only your voice could speak.

I wish I could see the proud look on your face
When I've done what I've always said I would do.
How I listened to you and stayed strong in this race
Overcoming every obstacle life will have taken me through.

I wish you could walk me down the church aisle
On the day when I marry the angel of my every dream.
I wish my children could know the love in your smile
And spend days with you making homemade ice cream.

I find comfort in knowing that you're happy and healthy now,

That your new destination was just part of life's journey.
All that you've instilled in me will help me make it somehow,
And one day I can join you again, where our spirits
can be free.

You will live forever in the stories I share,
You will love forever through me, in the way that I care.
I will pass on the lessons I have learned from you
And cherish every memory that I have of you, too.

Written by Ivana Monique
(daughter)
(July 12, 2003)

In Need Of A Friend

My heart was heavy, I knew not why.
I prayed, I fasted, and often cried.
Yet still my burdens just grew and grew,
The answer was somewhere, this I knew.

I searched just hoping to find someone
Along the path, I had just begun.
For I alone just could not bear,
To carry this burden one more year.

I've held it in for quite sometime
And only God could ease my mind.
When there was nothing I could do,
God helped me smile, my joy renew.

He understands when all else fails,
Through God I know I can prevail.
He tells me just to seek His face,
And He will help me run this race.

For He too, knew that on this earth
A burden soul must find some worth.
Yet friends had seemed to walk away,
So, on His shoulders my burdens lay.

Our friends they say, "depend on me,
I'm here for you, be worry free."
But words alone are all you hear,
When trouble comes, they disappear.

But it is grand to talk to God,
For He's a great, strong leaning rod.
Yet still a friend on earth you need;
Who understands your heart that bleeds!

My Savior cares, my Savior knows
A friend on earth can be a foe.
But He, Himself, set human pace
To talk to one of fleshly race.

He talked to God when things were rough,
And the world had made the going tough.
But He, too, had a friend in deed,
Who shared with Him in times of need.

This friend He had of earthly blood
Was one who had sustained the flood.
With him, He laughed, and talked and shared;
When death had come, He showed He cared.

And so, I search and as I go,
Another friend has turned a foe.
Oh Lord, I pour my heart to thee,
Who and where can this friend be?

My teacher, my pastor or some long lost kin,
The postman, the milkman, a carpenter then;
My sister, my brother, a loved one so fair,
Just let me know, somewhere, someone does care.

The Friend Who Just Stands By

When trouble comes your soul to try,
You thank the friend who just 'stands by.'
Perhaps there's nothing they can do;
This thing is strictly up to you.

The path you tread is all your own,
At times you travel it alone.
But God will help you bear the load,
As you travel down this road.

Yet knowing that you have a friend,
Who will 'stand by' you 'til the end;
Just seems to help you understand,
They will be there to hold your hand.

Somehow it helps to pull you through,
Although there's nothing they can do.
So, with a thankful heart you cry:
"God bless the friend who just 'stands by.'"

CPSIA information can be obtained
at www.ICGtesting.com
Printed in the USA
BVHW042111040521
606422BV00016B/182